CROSSING HOLY GROUND

A Desert Memoir In Poetic Form

CROSSING HOLY GROUND

A Desert Memoir In Poetic Form

D. G. AUGUSTYN

© 2025 by Dennis Augustyn
All Rights Reserved
No part of this book may be reproduced in any form or by any electronic or mechanical means including information storage and retrieval systems without permission in writing from the publisher, except by a reviewer who may quote brief passages in a review.

Sunstone books may be purchased for educational, business, or sales promotional use. For information please write: Special Markets Department, Sunstone Press, P.O. Box 2321, Santa Fe, New Mexico 87504-2321.
Printed on acid-free paper
∞
eBook: 978-1-61139-789-5

LIBRARY OF CONGRESS CATALOGING IN PUBLICATION DATA

(ON FILE)

WWW.SUNSTONEPRESS.COM
SUNSTONE PRESS / POST OFFICE BOX 2321 / SANTA FE, NM 87504-2321 /USA
(505) 988-4418

I leave and dedicate this book
To Renee and Jamie
With love and gratitude
For all they've done.
The best wine comes late.

And with
A Special tip of my hat
To Erika in all her
Tattooed splendor.

Here is a brief memoir
with strands of poetry and personal observations
woven through the fabric of language.
Reading this will not guarantee
Your spiritual perfection.

For that you must cross your own desert.
This thin work is only a guidebook
From one who has gone before you
Into the wilderness.
What I found there, is in these pages.

Origins

The anawim

The poor, the homeless, the misfits,

The outcasts, the lepers of our time.

I have lived the reality of these people and places.

I know those grim streets well,

Where despair is the daily milieu

Of the lost and despised.

Then I felt a spiritual nudge,

Or was it a push in the right direction?

I was to leave the city,

To flee for my life and my soul.

I resolved to go west, to follow the sun,

To find a light for my darkened heart.

And the desert called, "Come out to me."

INTERIOR

Then I entered an adobe chapel,

Not for the dark expose of confession,

But just to sit in the cool for a while.

I saw veiled women older than sandstone.

Their shaded faces like wind-scoured mesas,

Their dark eyes shuttered in prayer,

Their worn hands adorned with rosaries,

Fingers ticking off the decades.

"Santa Maria, Madre de Dios."

I felt like an intruder in this sacred place.

Yet as I followed their prayers,

Every woman became my Mother,

A deep spiritual bond formed,

In the interior of my heart.

I lit a candle before Our Lady of Guadalupe

And as I turned to leave, I heard,

"I've not forgotten you, my child."

ICONS

Lately every face I see shines like an Icon.
They bestow their weathered grace
Framed by misfortune,
Cheated by the vagaries of circumstance.
I love them for their crooked smiles,
The wounded iconography of living down and out.
If I could I'd fill their pockets with silver dollars.
Or better still, I'd pawn their battered halos
For a second chance at life.

STARSCAPE

You've never seen the stars until you stand in the desert.

Incomprehensible vastness opens before your eyes.

There is nothing superficial here.

You are looking at the deep eloquence of the Divine.

No words can convey the majesty.

A gasp, a sigh, a tear, silence.

You are privileged to have this night of sublime wonder

And for a moment to feel how small you are.

Perhaps there are voyagers racing across

The oceans of time and space

In gleaming ships searching for a signal

From that far, fair place called Home.

In Those Days

In those days when I drifted

Wherever some passing notion took me,

I lived by the nomad's rule of thumb -

"Where to? What next? Move on."

But in my transience, I longed for sanctuary,

A little down time from the demonic.

I followed the sun West into desert landscapes

Where the only relief I found was in dusty,

Sweltering Mexican villages with their ancient poverty.

The Bedouins of Arabia have a saying,

"The desert is where God comes to rest."

There are stories of desert bandits who became

Great holy men and repentant prostitutes

Washing the feet of weary travelers.

And how many anonymous monks

have skittered across the burning sands?

In those days I was in exile.

I had abandoned the place of my birth

For I had become a stranger

in the very culture that had bred me.

The city I once called home had disintegrated into chaos.

There was nothing perverse or

Corrupt that was not permissible.

Squalor filled the streets with

Legions of destitute, dangerous men. And so, I left a refugee.

In those days on moonless nights

I sped past towns like islands of light,

An archipelago of life flickering

In the black expanse of desert nothingness.

In those parched wastes, coyotes chorus

The fall of civilization.

Men come with their machines to scratch

Their histories on the earth and then destroy themselves.

The desert buries the victors and the victims,

Side by side.

Epiphany!

I am a man of little consequence

With neither lofty credentials to boast

Of nor the slightest achievement,

No matter how modest,

To proclaim my spiritual worth.

And yet, there are moments when I'm filled

With such an exquisite ache

Of beauty and tender longing

That I can't help but fling the curtains

Of my narrow understanding

Wider than the confines of my mind's shabby room

To more perfectly embrace the sublime wonder

Of Christ's boundless and unconditional Love.

FALLEN ANGELS

In the clear, cold light of day,

We're all liars turned authors.

But once, long ago,

Our thoughts had wings

And we were beautiful.

So how did we fall

Into this disgrace?

Our error was trusting

Our own powers.

Alas, we were always

Such vain creatures.

Ordinary Days

Old friends have traveled on

By death or other conveyance.

My only child won't speak to me.

I've quit going into town.

I don't care to hear the gossip.

After eighty years all my sermonizing

Has softened to a serenade.

I polish poems found

Like sapphires in the mud

Sometimes I just sit by the river

Alone with the ALONE.

The cities are dead zones

I whistle a Requiem.

Did I mention that I pray more these days?

Death Watch

I held her hand looking down at the woman

Who'd given me life. Mother.

At this stage doctors are pointless.

The dying need a Priest

To restore their souls to God.

All hospitals have a room

Set aside for the terminal.

A bed, a chair or two, and a morphine drip

Feeding oblivion into desiccated veins.

She had suffered many

Disappointments in her time.

At the end I think she just wanted us to be happy.

I kissed her goodnight.

There should have been an angel.

I closed her eyes.

The Dance

Let us dance the Tango of life

While the band swings with beatific rhythms.

Let's hold each other tight

Until two breathe as one.

Let us hurl caution to the wind

For the passion in our blood demands

That we live every moment.

And the music we follow flows

Like a river through canyons

Deep in our memories

Where ancient dancers have gone before us

Teaching us the turns, the dips, the twirls of life

Until an Angel with violet eyes

Taps us on our shoulders and smiles,

"May I have this dance?"

MARTYRS

Give me the persecuted ones,

Those scourged with addictions,

Ravaged by madness,

Crowned with contempt,

And crucified by public opinion.

Give me the defiant ones

Who stand apart

And sing hosannas

Into the jaws of lions.

CHARLIE

Another reservation dawn.

The tribal land is a mockery of

Broken promises and maimed lives.

The Pueblo is a monument to

Heroic survival from pre-history

To the arrival of

Steel, gunpowder, and whiskey.

Charlie slumps on the ragged seat

Of an abandoned car, dozing in boozy oblivion

From a quart of Old Crow.

In another life Charlie rises from his drunken stupor

To walk with Eagle feathers in his hair,

Turquoise around his neck and wrists,

An elder honored by his people

And sung about in the stories of his tribe.

MY WAY

I'll never go back but

I'll never forget where I came from.

The past is mired in tears and sorrows.

There's a lesson here.

Live long enough and

You'll learn to laugh.

Your sanity will demand it.

And of all the folly and

Foolishness around,

Learn to laugh at yourself first.

So if you pass my way

Stop and say hello.

I'll be the one with a

Clown's face painted on.

The Good We Do

Take your coat

From the hook on the door.

Let's walk outside

On this wintry night.

Let's pretend that life is fair,

That widows and orphans

Are well fed,

That the homeless

Find warm beds,

That the lonely are

Embraced by friends,

That Angels

comfort the sick and dying,

And the prisoners go free.

We know it's not true

but for tonight,

Let's do what we can for them.

Eclipse

Maybe death is a

String of Christmas lights

Winking on and off.

You haven't touched your

Novel in months.

What are you waiting for?

Get busy living.

Your life is the masterpiece.

The sky is darkening

As I write this.

The birds

Have fallen silent.

Death is only an eclipse.

I'll see you on the bright side.

        10/14/23

Morning Coffee

It's five-thirty in the morning.

I'm sitting at the

Kitchen table in the dark.

Distant thunder.

I have an eerie feeling

That I'm not alone.

I scan the perimeter of the room.

Nothing out of the ordinary.

I'm alone on a small blue planet

Circling an average star

Out on the rim of a spiral galaxy.

I pour a cup of coffee

For myself and fill one

For the guest who isn't there.

The Chosen

They burned the synagogues first.

Always the Jew first.

With gloved hand the officer

Aimed his pistol

At the back of a head.

Only Jews fit for work were spared.

Arbeit Macht Frei!!

Rooms full of shoes. Bales of human hair.

And where was there

beauty enough to transcend the pain.

Transforming such horror into exaltation?

Where was the hand of God

To stop this evil?

Hear O Israel lamentations

In the camps where your children were

Slaughtered like Paschal lambs.

WARSAW '39

And the poets of Warsaw

Ran into the streets waving

Their slim books of verse

Like paper sabers against

German tanks.

Didn't they know that

Words are not stronger than steel?

Bullets wrote in blood

Upon those immortals.

Whose poems still live

In Polish hearts.

Some things cannot be killed.

HIROSHIMA '45

The cranes are dancing

In Hiroshima.

Buddha sits serenely in the park.

It's time to extinguish

The night lanterns.

But wait.

No need to rush.

Her heart is my lantern

Let it glow a little longer.

See how lovely she looks

In her willow kimono.

She turns to see if I'm looking.

How many eyes on a peacock's tail?

At least that many.

I follow her discreetly.

She pretends not to see me.

It's a love game we play.

And then a white chrysanthemum

flashes in the sky.

She vanishes in a blinding light.

I search the

Blasted city for days.

Crushing love blown down

Beneath my feet like reeds in a storm.

And where I last heard

Her playful laughter,

I find only her shadow

On a garden wall.

Desert Prayer

Praise to You O Lord of the Desert

Who wills all life to thrive-

The sand fleas in my blanket,

The scorpion in my boot and

This cactus thorn in my finger.

Ah, but you are my guide to sweet water,

To fat quail for my pan and

Honey in the comb.

And when the sun dips below the hills

I rest in your shade until

Nightfall folds me in dreams.

So, I turn to you,

Holy One,

As I sit by the side of the road

Tossing pebbles at passing devils.

A Subversive Poem

I am a scarecrow

Made of discarded dreams.

Overlooking desert ruins

Where a thousand years ago,

Sweet water flowed.

I am a free desperado in the

Well-oiled machine,

Where the tyranny of the

Status quo crushes Holy curiosity.

Question everything.

Defend what beauty remains.

Be kind to scarecrows.

Epiphany 2

If I had lived an exotic life in

Some elegant story,

Stepping from a sleek carriage into

A brilliant party-colored world

Instead of running down alleys

In the dark nights of my soul.

Howling my poems

To a mob that cares

Nothing for subtlety

But only the show.

Then, then,

I would never have stepped

Into that church, that peace,

That Presence,

And heard my name called.

Second Coming

What if Christ comes back this week?

Will it be on the day of your

Appointment with the therapist?

Or maybe you'll be

Stuck in traffic with a migraine?

Will you even know?

Yes, there could be phenomena –

Earthquakes, tsunamis,

Meteors falling,

The dead rising from their graves.

But what if it were just the two of you?

And He knew your name.

Could you look Him in the eyes?

Could you hold back your tears?

Monk

To give everything away.
To finally own nothing.
To take up as little space
In the world as possible.

To stand before GOD.
To be able to say,
"I have only my heart left to give."

Artist

The desert is full of inspiration.
If it doesn't sting you, bite you, or
Poison your liver,
You may create something sublime.

I held a 1000-year-old clay pot
From a dig in Sierra County.
The pot was painted inside and out
With a menagerie of fantastic creatures.
The artist who made it won
No blue ribbon at the county fair.
But ten centuries ago
She carried hot beans and flat bread
To her family.
They were all smiles.

The Message

For tens of thousands of years

The snows have come in season

To blanket the sleeping earth,

To speak softly in a language

We've almost forgotten.

Each flake that falls is a

Single letter in the message.

And as if they were written in code,

They melt in the palm of your hand.

You step outside.

The rush of cold air condenses your

Warm breath into plumes of mist.

A gold foil box is on your doorstep

No address, no return.

You lift off the cover and find three perfect red, ripe apples.

Is it an anonymous gift or another part of the message?

TO THE GATEKEEPER

Look.

It's like this.

No one is perfect.

Sometimes, often,

We go astray.

We get lost.

Our lives are full of

Crooked paths and wrong turns.

It may take years

Before we find our way back.

And those who arrive late are

The ones who've travelled the farthest.

God is merciful.

Let them pass.

HAVEN

I'm imagining a small adobe house

Beside a jump over stream.

There's an old cottonwood tree

Split by lightning, still green.

I dig a fire pit out back

And line it with found stones.

A few good friends

Drop over in the evenings.

The ladies always bring

Something delicious.

There's always a guitar or

Accordion or native flute.

And Senorita Maria Lopez

Always asks me to dance.

I let her lead.

She's only a child of twelve.

Morning Comes

I face the rising sun with arms wide open.
At day's beginning my mind is
Still free of distractions,
My heart receptive.
I begin anew.
I meditate on the desert's
Ageless mysteries as it unfolds the
Canticles of Creation
In an iridescent green beetle
Inching its way over the
Crystal glimmering sand
Scattered by the invisible hand of the wind.
And I stand in God's field of view as
He shakes out the night's blanket
Throwing light across the desert.

BLESSINGS

Bless you on the lonesome road.

Bless you tossing on the sea.

Bless you in harm's way

From oaths and lies and evil doers.

Bless you with warm

Hearths in the grip of winter.

Bless you with friends as

True as silver bells.

Bless you with an

Angel's share in your glass and

Bless you when you find a loving home.

For truly you have found a life worth living.

In Retrospect

I was born on June 30th, 1941,

To a Polish Catholic family in Chicago.

What else would you like to know?

That I've lived now for over 80 years

Is a source of amazement to me.

I must be a real hard case for

God to devote so much patience

To my rehabilitation.

Either that, or the Devil much

Enjoys my company and is loath to leave.

We calculate the worth of our works and days not,

I would hope, with only the cold deliberations of our minds,

But with the familial kindness of our humanity.

For when we've touched our deepest chords,

We resonate together in harmony

That's like Adoration of

The One by Whose word, all things exist.

WHO'S TO SAY?

A sailboat rounds the strand, with all pennants flying.

It is Rome come to rescue the mystic from his religious delusions.

When the mystic sees the boat turn toward the shore,

He runs down to the beach frantically waving his arms.

"No! No! Not yet. Away with you! The visions are still coming."

The anchor drops. The sails are furled.

And a party of prelates rows ashore.

The mystic hides himself

In the figure of Christ crucified.

But they find him by following the blood.

They coax the mystic down from the cross

With crumbs of sweet theology.

He is now mopping floors

In a monastery, doing penance.

And once in a while they still catch him glowing in the dark.

American Gothic

A row of folding chairs,
Each with a cushion of new snow,
Beside an open grave.
The coffin sits in the trench
Ready to be shoveled over.
In the spring they'll
Auction off his equipment.
The farm has already been
Sold to developers.
His children have
Driven back to the city.
No one has stayed behind
In the old house to remember.
On the gate down by the road
A tin sign rattles in the wind.
No Trespassing!

The Time Before

It's beyond human memory

In a time before Time,

They huddle together

In a circle, and within the circle,

A ring of stones and a fire.

We don't know Their names.

They were 'The People'.

The old ones told stories.

Their words blew away

On the wind.

The nights were long

And O' how they

Feared the dark.

Allison whispers to me,

"Throw another log on the fire."

Heart to Heart

An idea cannot be killed

Once established in the heart.

It can be denied

Or crushed

And still it will spread

From heart to heart.

Jesus came, Emmanuel,

And men doubted,

Demanding some proof,

Something that only God could do

—like dying on the cross and

a resurrection -

This is our Faith.

He lives in our hearts

And always will.

THE ASCENT

1. Looking out from the trail at about six thousand feet up. I could see for a hundred miles. The river below was a thin green rope snaking its way south to the Gulf of Mexico. The desert hadn't changed for centuries. From this altitude you can still detect the outlines of early settlements, just traces of adobe in the sand, crumbling walls and seared timbers.

2. I had reached the frontier of a spiritual country. "Come out to me." The desert had called, as I shed the sinister agendas of the city of my birth. Below me in the wide, timeless expanse of the desert, there was something more than an arid landscape. It's in the light that dazzles the eye like a sacrament chased in gold. It is pure, holy and radiant with the Glory of God.

3. A pathway opened for me on the mountain, a clearly defined passage that had begun in darkness a thousand miles away, and years ago, in the discontent of my former days. I became aware of a Presence who had gathered the fragments of my life assuring me that I would be made whole again. "I will give you a new heart, and a new spirit I will put within you." And my tears flowed with streams of mercy.

4. And in my ancient sorrows a new celebration began. From its hidden den in the rocks a cougar roared. A pair of red tail hawks' dove from the heights in pirouettes. A turtle bumped along; its mottled shell still wet with dew. All the hum and bustle of life's continuity gave praise for the gift of being each according to its kind. And I stood in the gilded hall of morning before a Throne of Light.

5. To see ourselves as we really are, is a bitter drink. But it can be a healing draft. No, I am not beautiful. I lack symmetry. The older I become the more imperfections I see. I no longer concern myself with appearances. Perfection belongs to God. But if I could, I'd sip from the cup of His Beauty and let it burn away all the ugliness that I have wrought in this life.

6. A new man came down from that mountain. A changed man. For the promise made to me had been fulfilled. My 'heart of stone was plucked out and replaced with a heart of flesh.' And a new spirit burned within me. There was nothing extraordinary in my appearance. But inward the charnel house of my past had been purged of corruption by a cleansing fire.

7. Zephyr. An old word meaning a gentle breeze. A zephyr caresses the sleeping infant cradled in his mother's arms. Haven't we all seen this image, Madonna and Child? It's on our Christmas cards. And when she gave her fiat, "Let it be done unto me," Oh how the angels must have rejoiced with heavenly zephyrs from their wings, caressing this girl who would be the Mother of our Lord.

8. They come to the desert seeking spiritual wisdom. And any old man with a dusty beard and worn-out sandals becomes their Abba. I've walked desert trails for twenty years and I've met plenty of devils. But when asked for the whereabouts of a genuine Desert Father, I direct them to that great mystical saint pumping gas at a station down the road. But you can't get there from here.

9. In tears flow streams of mercy and in sorrow forgiveness begins. In the desert we embrace simplicity and walk humbly before our God. We pray from the book of our heart and live by the work of our hands. We commend the world to the care of the Lord but expect each day its end.

10. I came to New Mexico to find a life
unobstructed by a society that diminishes
and ultimately obliterates the soul.
I was drawn to the desert because
I believed that the stark lay of the land
was the anvil on which the Holy Spirit
hammered our scraps into eternal patterns.
And I entered the furnace
and found the Heart of God ablaze with Love.
I was alone with the Alone in Whom all things exist.

The Disciple

His message was not well received.

He told them what his Teacher had said.

They laughed at him. They spit.

They mocked his gospel.

They hurled insults and objects.

He left that town in the dust.

These people preferred their own

Comfortable idolatries.

They needed no new revelation.

They never doubted the old gods.

They had no reason to question.

Things were the way they were and that was that.

And yet, what if there was

Something more in what he said?

A few of them wanted to hear it all.

They followed him.

Fragment

Who is that man

coming down the way?

I think I knew him once

but that was far away,

Before the world laid siege to my life

and I surrendered.

Is it He who loved me then

and has not forgotten?

He who has kept his covenant

in blood poured out for me?

Here I am Lord.

A Door Open to Morning

People said that he'd

Never amount to much

And they were right.

But just this once

He strides across

A golden carpet of sunlight.

He crosses the floor like

The Emperor of Morning.

Crucified

The hammer slammed down again and again

Driving the six-inch spikes into His flesh,

Nailing His wrists to the crossbeam.

He cried out in agony. Another spike longer,

Was hammered through His feet.

He groaned, for the pain was excruciating.

Blood poured down the cross pooling at its base.

Sweat saturated His body stinging the wounds

From the hundred lashes, His tormenters had savagely applied.

And the wicked thorns encircling His brow crowned His Divinity.

About three in the afternoon, He spoke his last.

"It is finished." His head dropped and He died.

A Roman soldier stabbed Him with a lance

To ensure that no life remained

And in three days He walked out of the tomb.

"It is to be believed because it is absurd."   Tertullian

Siren Song

I was a boy of fifteen fishing for
Bluegills and croppies off the pier at Seminary Lake.
But my attention was on that girl in the water
Just offshore, her voice transcending my boyish world.
If I could have stopped time, that summer
Would never have ended.
But then, I wouldn't be here to tell this story.
There was a promise in her song
Too good to be true.
She knew I was listening and drew me on over
Into waters dangerous for a boy who couldn't
Swim in her currents.
I ran home and flew a kite
In the afternoon breeze.
Like the sail of Odysseus' ship bound for Ithaca.

The Book Lover

The quality of the light in autumn

Is like looking through smoky glass.

Perhaps it's the golden

Parchment of fallen leaves

Burning in backyards like

The Library of Alexandria.

Such rare tomes should be

Kept In locked boxes and only

Brought out on rainy days.

October is my favorite month.

I rake the fragments of

Oaks and elms and Sophocles.

The Cloisters

Schoolgirls come laughing
Past a fountain in the
Courtyard of a convent.
The fountain shoots a
Spray of sun-dazzled water
Into the morning.
The spray drifts on a breeze
Over a bed of red and yellow tulips
Settling in a mist over
The graves of long deceased nuns,
Row after row of white crosses
Like exclamation points
To hidden lives.

The Pearl

A tear drops like a pearl into the indigo night.

Smoke from a cigarette curls like a blue oracle.

She expected too much, the world is finite.

The empire of love is burning to ashes.

Paper roses have no fragrance and no thorns.

She prefers the flowers of solitude out of pain.

Something she's lived to lay on the altar.

Her broken soiled heart, a pearl of great price.

FRAGMENT

His right hand is palsied.

He is legally blind.

He walks with the

Aid of a brace on his leg.

Precise work is

Unlikely to ever

Leave his mind.

But oh, how that boy can sing!

Ancestors

What would I say to those who came before me?

How far back must I look to recognize

The origins of this brief pageant of my life?

They are here, locked in this mortal flesh,

Every ancient nuance of my temperament

Written in genetic code, a gift or an affliction.

Would I be as foreign to them as they seem to me now,

Though our blood is mingled somehow.

Were they only illiterate peasants or did they sire kings?

Are their graves weathered to nothing

Or do they sleep beneath cold cathedral stones

Where swarms of tourists scuff their noble bones?

And I alone am left with ink and quill to speculate.

I feel a kinship with the past, those lives who went before,

like the distant prologue to a family.

Sacred Music

The Sacred

lives in the world

but men ignore it.

It hides between the

Shopping mall and the

Sports stadium.

It hums its melodic theme

Above the roar of the crowd.

And the crowd turns up the

Volume of their

Latest hit tune,

Deaf to the music of

Creation of which

They are the passing notes.

Fragments

When traditions are lost,

We lose our identity.

When the better angels

Of our past are forgotten,

We create the monsters

Of our future.

Weeds grow in the cracks

And walls fall down.

Conversion

I watched a small

Gray moth fly in circles

Around and around

A candle in the dark

Drawing closer and closer.

To the mystery of the light.

Until it became

One with the flame.

Claiming Heaven

Who can claim Heaven?
Only those who've been bitten by the world
Or those who've failed at everything.
Only those who are just too old, sick, and tired
To carry a load of guilt anymore.
Only those ready to let go of everything
And give it back to God.

First and last cause.
The prime Mover and Shaker of our lives,
Dwells in that place where you feel most
Abandoned and forsaken, when you come
To a precipice and a taunting voice says,
"Go ahead jump!" But you turn away.
"Not yet. Not yet."

Then and only then will the bitter
Waters of living sweeten in your
Mouth like a rare vintage.

Then and only then will a troupe of ragtag angels
Lead you dancing through the gates.

Then and only then will your tears
Be wiped away, replaced by laughter.

Then and only then will you be escorted
To the place reserved for you at this your wedding banquet.

Then and only then can you claim
Heaven as your own.

Fragment

After a spiritual skirmish

I examine my soul

Counting bruises.

Some days there are only one or two.

At other times I'm a map of wounds.

The devil gives no quarter.

I ask for no terms.

The war goes on.

World Without End

Martin Luther was asked,

"What if someone told you

That the end of the world was near?

What would you do?"

Luther replied, "I'd plant a tree."

Winter's imperative

Loses its grip and the sap begins to flow.

The cambium swells with the sweet liquor of life

Beneath the bark and the roots pulse with tomorrow.

Upon every branch green buds wait in secret intrigue

With the sun until, as if on cue, they break winter's

Icy hold with the riot of another spring.

Fragment

At the trinity site in New Mexico,
I walked in the residual radiation
Of the first A-Bomb test in 1945.

Vendors sold T-shirts
Picturing the Apocalypse.
O spacious skies.

On Borrowed Time

The party balloons deflate and shrivel

In the corners of the room

Like puckered old widows

Under sediments of rouge and thick mascara.

The bored entertainer packs up his accordion

Slipping the hundred-dollar bill

Into his vest pocket.

The guests drop their paper party hats

In the stairwell shedding motes of glitter

On the steps like lies of eternal youth.

It's not wise to celebrate a birthday after seventy-five.

Too many unanswered charges.

Better to have a quiet drink on the rooftop,

Feed cake to the pigeons and

Watch the sunset without fanfare.

The Interview

What do you want most?

To be young again.

Be realistic.

What do you really want?

To know if my life made any difference.

Is that all or is there more?

To reconcile with those I've injured.

Anything else?

Will my name appear in your report?

No. You've been assigned a number.

I insist that you use my name.

No one has a name here.

It confuses the machines.

Not a Saint

I am no doe-eyed plaster saint
With tenure in my niche.

I'm an irregular disciple
Who must begin anew each day.

I sin and confess
And do it again.

Alas, I detect the odor of sulfur.

Pray for me
As I will for you.

It's later than we think.

A Book Review

A dictator had all his speeches

Written in a book for posterity.

The pages were of finest vellum.

The text had gilded capitals

Delicately laid on by highly skilled scribes.

His smiling faced appeared

On the title page circled by a

Wreath of wide-eyed children.

Of course, the thing was a travesty,

A graveyard of lies bound between

Rich leather covers.

His opus was required reading.

The Ministry of Culture printed a million copies.

I used the pages to line the bottoms of bird cages.

Birds do make a mess. I change the pages twice a week.

FRAGMENTS

If you want to hear Beauty

Listen to the Fantasy Overture

Of Tchaikovsky's Romeo and Juliet.

And if you don't hear it

You're a stone

At the bottom of a dry well.

A Walk in the Park

A black dog

Is following me.

When I stop, it stops.

I hide behind a tree

And it's there, waiting.

If I was superstitious

I'd think it was

A demon from hell.

I throw a stone at it. "Go away."

It snarls showing its yellow teeth.

Then a kid sidles up next to me.

"Don't be afraid mister."

He stares deeply into the dog's eyes.

"He grins before he bites,

Just like people."

FATHER MIKE

"You shall love the Lord your God
With all your heart, with all your soul,
With all your mind and with all your strength.
And you shall love your neighbor as yourself."
{Mark 12:30-31}

"If you want to please God,
If you want to go to heaven,
Here's the way.
It's as simple as this."
Father Mike walked back
To his seat and said no more.

JUST THIS

I would like to be loved in my old age.

I would like to give her my hand

And be shown her hideaway

Where she keeps her woman's secrets.

I'd like to touch her as if she were

a mysterious island with undiscovered passions.

What does it mean to be human

If not to give and receive the warmth of a warm heart?

I would like to wake up in her arms

With sunlight streaming through white curtains.

Just this,

Before the cold earth opens to receive me.

Fragment

If you're on the fast track
To hell you will come to a
Crossing that may be
Your last chance
To jump free.
You'll know the place is near
When your heart
Feels lighter than air.
O, the devil
will try to snatch you back.
But you belong to the sky now.
Fly away little bird.
Fly away home.

LISTENING

Lately, the sounds of living have

Become more important to me

Then the incessant chatter of my mind.

I'm hearing the world all around me –

A hammer pounding nails,

A baby bawling for its mother,

A plumber banging pipes

In the subterranean depths,

A woman singing as she hangs out the wash,

A freight train calling on the plains

For miles where the wind hums

Through the tall grass.

Sounds are heralds from the borders of our lives.

Sounds will tell you things before they happen.

Are you listening?

Fragment

When adolescent hearts touch

There are fireworks.

When seasoned hearts join together

A sea of understanding flows into each.

Then the two become one, or drift apart.

But don't we sometimes miss the fireworks?

Doubt

So many doubts

Go unanswered.

We stammer into

The distance and hear

Our own echoes come back.

Give us just one intimate

Conversation, a small

Voice passing through

Time, just a breath

To surround our

Loneliness so that we

May know you are there.

Communion

I taste the Eucharist.

The Holy morsel dissolves

On my tongue.

Bread into His body.

Wine becomes His blood.

Don't ask me how.

I accept the mystery of His Presence.

I want to weep.

I want to laugh.

I tremble.

Blackwell

Twenty years in prison. As he described it,

His conversion was a process,

A slow coming to Christ in a cage of stone and steel.

"You adapt to your surroundings, or you go mad."

One day bleeds into next. The routine never changes.

There are rules and punishments for infractions.

"The guards are sadistic bastards."

Blackwell told me of the night his world shifted.

His cellmate was passed out from too much hooch.

And for some reason the guard missed his usual rounds.

When he looked through the bars, he saw

A figure clothed in light so bright it brought tears to his eyes.

"John" the figure spoke. "Are you ready?"

He was free at last.

NATIVITY

The tides will roll on.

Sun and moon will cross the sky.

Days follow nights

Cities will burn and crumble.

Centuries will pass

Unrecorded.

Then in some remote future

When the past is smoke and myths,

A man and woman

Will huddle in the ruins of a church

And She will go into Labor.

Epiphany 3

I was down for the count, bruised but not beaten.

One more contender for glory on the streets of Chicago.

Not to be—eight, nine, ten. You're out! Things were bleak.

I walked the streets in aimless confusion.

Then, as if to ease my troubled soul,

And reassure my spirit.

I saw this message on a signboard

Above a laundromat.

"For I know the plans I have for you."

Declares the Lord.

"Plans to prosper you and not to harm you,

Plans to give you hope and a future."

                                    Jeremiah 29:11

Fragment

Life is a gift,

Savor your days

Whether fat or lean.

Spend each moment as if it

Were money, and celebrate

Your years.

If you have a bottle of wine

Bring it.

Invite your favorite,

There will be guitars.

And give thanks to God

For you're still alive

And you're not in jail.

The Prophet At Home

No one wants

to hear him anymore.

They never understood

his cryptic babbling.

What the Almighty told him

He keeps locked in his heart.

He tried.

They wouldn't listen.

He tends to his trees.

He brings in the harvest.

His wife is weaving

A new winter blanket

When the Voice

Comes to him from out of a cloud.

"Go!"

The Penitent

My days have settled

Like snow on ruins

Full of ancient memories.

There is no praise or blame.

Time has erased the particulars.

I am only a man whose

Story remains a remnant

Of his seasons on Earth.

I spoke in the old tongue

Of love, death, and God.

And I left my soul open

For the radiance of angels.

THE FEEDING

At dawn the man empties a sack

Of apples into a metal trough.

The forest is listening.

Deer appear from the tree line

And gather in the meadow

Guarded by a twelve-point buck.

They cautiously approach the trough's sweet bounty.

The buck rakes the ground with his antlers.

A warning. A challenge, eye to eye.

The man yields the right of way

Then wisely retreats a dozen paces.

The deer circle the trough and dig into the feast.

The man smells coffee and bacon from the house.

His wife leans out of the screen door and calls, "John, breakfast."

Like phantoms the deer vanish into the morning mist.

Fragment

This book is where

I've left my best,

My joy and

my sorrows.

And all of it

Directed

by the Holy Spirit

To His purpose.

Praise Him!

Ghosts

Ghosts no longer haunt my mind

With their translucent antics.

Grasping at me for one

More fling in my flesh.

It is finished my friends,

Whoever you were.

It's the one consolation

Of growing old,

We're allowed to forget.

Hello. Goodbye. I knew you when?

What we've lived, suffered,

has been written in The Book of Life.

The Akashic Record knows our strife.

Go spook some other sinner.

I scare myself enough.

Fragment

It saddens me to see

How many people believe

That this life is all we have.

We are souls in temporary bodies.

Souls alive for eternity.

When you can't see beyond

The physical,

You are truly dead

Though you linger.

TO THE FUGITIVE

You're on the run, a wanted man.

They burned down your house

And carried off your wife and children.

There's a price on your head.

You can't go back ever.

Flee to the desert wilderness.

Disguise yourself as

One of the half-starved monks.

They too are wanted men.

No one knows their names or where they came from.

And they won't tell. Learn from them.

Keep your mouth shut and your eyes open.

Choose an alias to be known by.

I am the 'Scarecrow.'

Welcome to the brotherhood.

CHRISTIANS

The pilgrimage of the heart

Is going out from ourselves,

A martyrdom of self-interest.

It's the cross each of us must carry

In our particular circumstance.

It's to pray without ceasing

By the lives we live.

Let them see how

We love one another.

From Eden's Gates

Come together.

Rejoice in being alive for each other.

Defend your love against the sinister forces

Of those intellectual charlatans who would

Lure you into cavernous doubts

As to who and what you are.

No power on earth can override

What lives in your soul.

You were created as a man or woman,

Not interchangeable, not transitional,

But as the singular beauty of being yourselves,

Unique expressions of the unvarying ethos of God.

You were fashioned distinctly

As male or female in His plan before

We invented civilization with all its psychoses.

You are not an accident.

You are not

an alien experiment in eugenics.

You are a woman or a man,

Not a prisoner trapped

In the wrong gender.

Human nature has not

Fundamentally changed

Since we left the gates of Eden

On our journey to here and now.

A Renaissance Man

I am looking through a dirty window

Out onto a street wet with dirty snow.

A foul mist hangs low over the city

And the air I breathe is chemical.

But what if I were in Tuscany lounging

In a Renaissance Villa gilded with a

Thousand years of warm Italian sun?

What if workers were singing

In the olive groves and a stream

Of red wine flowed from an ancient

Grotto in the hills filling my glass

With the blood of the earth?

Suppose I'm courting a Contessa,

From a noble Roman family and

Another suitor throws down his gauntlet.

I could stay and fight. I could let her go.

Or claim sanctuary in a church.

But the priest would require a confession

And what if someone overheard?

I might as well broadcast my sins

Over loudspeakers. A tragedy. A comedy.

I'd slip away to Paris, City of Lights,

Where starving artists kneel in the

Palace of the Louvre to worship

The ideal of Beauty, a Parisian past time,

Degas, Monet, Renoir, and Cezanne,

The delicate balance of Notre Dame.

Cocktails at seven, dinner at eight,

Before the iron rain falls from

The bellies of bombers and

Beauty, Art, and Civilization are

Blown into the darkness again.

EPILOGUE

Only those born into

A warring century

Can know the anguish

Of living for the moment

For there may not

Be a tomorrow.

I scan the night sky waiting

For the first silver light

Of dawn to confirm

That our hope is valid,

That morning will come,

And that we have survived

To raise from the ashes.

A new Renaissance.

Fragment

Question everything
In the light of your reason.
But remember
Pascal's famous remark,
"The heart has its reasons
Of which reason knows nothing."
Love cannot be purchased
But only lost and found.
It's not a thing to be
Possessed but only passed around.

The Month Of Winds

How inadequate words are.

How elusive the One I seek.

There's no technique to master.

You might as well try

Scooping up sand with a net.

My prayers are contrived,

Heat without light.

I can do nothing today

But wait out the wind

Listening for whispers.

By Love Alone

On page 50

Of Willa Cather's novel,

'Death Comes For

The Archbishop'

She writes through the voice

Of Father Vaillant that our

Perceptions are made finer

By the infusion of God's love

And that by this divine gift

We can recognize miracles.

Then and Now

It was a moonless night

When the bus pulled into town.

It was late, or early in the a.m.

If you look at time that way.

Of course, the streets were deserted.

Not even a stray dog.

There was some wind,

A dry warm kiss from the desert.

'Welcome to nowhere.'

I looked for an all-night diner.

Darkness.

'Why here?', I asked the wind.

'Of all the purgatories I could have come to.

Why this?' God's ways are inscrutable.

I intended to leave for California.

But I'd heard that California was populated

By decaying starlets and burnt-out dreams.

There's something to be said for small desert towns.

They have a lively Mexican church here and a bookstore.

I think I'll stay.

That was a quarter century ago.

I've grown old here.

I remain in the pews praying

And my rooms are full of half-read books.

Everyone knows my name.

Some wave on the street and some don't.

And sometimes I still walk out to the highway

And look a long way off.

THE LEGACY

Our people came through great hardships.

They died by the thousands from cold,

Hunger, disease and wars.

Only those of great spiritual stamina survived.

They transferred the knowledge

And wisdom of centuries to their children

Who in their turn created a new

Golden age and then destroyed it.

Leaving fragments of their civilization

To be pieced together by historians,

But are better told by poets

And story tellers around

the night fires of our tribe.

I lift my glass to those writers, poets,

And myth makers who keep the fires

Of our species burning on their lips

For as long as there's someone to listen.

The Welsh poet Dylan Thomas wrote,

"Do not go gentle into that good night,

But rage, rage against the dying of the light…"

And there it is, our work and our vocation,

To keep the light of Truth, Beauty,

And Goodness alive and to pass it on,

If anyone's left to receive it.

                        D.G.A.

AFTERWORD

In February of 1540,

The Coronado expedition set out

To find and conquer

The Seven Cities of Cibola

Rumored to be the storehouses

Of vast riches.

Of course,

They discovered only dusty pueblos,

Hostile natives, disillusionment

And death along the way.

After two years of failure,

Coronado called it quits

Returning to Compostela

In disgrace ending

His days, twelve years later,

A broken and forgotten man.

New Mexico,

This poor, bloody land,

Its history a dirge

Of martyrdoms and massacres.

And yet, there is such beauty
In the arid landscape
That one can believe
That this is where
God comes to rest.
It is the spiritual frontier.
I have chosen
Not to dwell on the atrocities
Committed against the Indians
By the conquistadors,
But instead to remember
The Black Robes, (Jesuits),
And Brown Robes, (Franciscans),
Who risked their lives
To bring the Gospel
To the indigenous
People of the Southwest.
The measure of their success
Can be seen in the predominance
Of the Catholic Church
In Hispanic culture.
And for that I say,
"Viva Espana!"

A Personal Note

To hold a tenderness

For all living things.

To place yourself last

In the service of others.

To be still and know

God is near.

To pray with your life

And not just words.

Blessed are those

Who love God,

Who labor in the vineyards

For the Kingdom.

Thank you Renee.
      —Dennis

www.ingramcontent.com/pod-product-compliance
Lightning Source LLC
Chambersburg PA
CBHW011955150426
43199CB00020B/2872